50 NIFTY™

Space Aliens
TO
DRAW

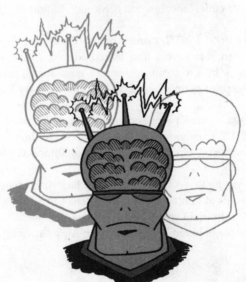

Written and illustrated by Neal Yamamoto
Drawing instructions by Jessica Oifer

LOWELL HOUSE JUVENILE

LOS ANGELES

NTC/Contemporary Publishing Group

NOTE: The numbered eraser in the upper right-hand corner of each project indicates the level of difficulty—1 being the easiest and 3 the hardest.

Published by Lowell House
A division of NTC/Contemporary Publishing Group, Inc.
4255 West Touhy Avenue, Lincolnwood (Chicago), Illinois 60646-1975 U.S.A.

Managing Director and Publisher: Jack Artenstein
Director of Publishing Services: Rena Copperman
Editorial Director: Brenda Pope-Ostrow
Director of Juvenile Development: Amy Downing
Designer: Bret Perry
Typesetter: C. Wendt

Library of Congress Catalog Card Number: 98-75611
ISBN 0-7373-0163-5

Lowell House books can be purchased at special discounts
when ordered in bulk for premiums and special sales.
Contact Customer Service at the above address,
or call 1-800-323-4900.

Printed and bound in the United States of America
10 9 8 7 6 5 4 3 2 1

Contents

Icthyopian

ADD YOUR OWN SCALY BODY TO THIS LIQUID-DWELLING ALIEN.

1. Draw an oval for the alien's head. Add two pointed ears, and then begin to create its eyes.

2. Complete its eyes, and sketch its mouth.

3. Add three *V*s for its scaly nose. Sketch a fin on top of its head.

4. Draw pupils in its eyes, and sketch the neck and shoulders. Begin to add scales on the fin and ears.

5. Continue to detail, adding rounded scales on the alien's forehead and angled lines down its neck.

6. Erase the unneeded lines. Then finish your Icthyopian by filling in its pupils and mouth. Also, add more scales around its face.

4

Barimite

THE BARIMITE USES ITS LONG POINTED LEGS TO SPEAR PREDATORS THAT LIVE ON ITS WILD PLANET.

1. First, draw a large circle for the Barimite's head. Add two eyes and a down-turned mouth.

2. Add its two pointed front legs. Then sketch a tuft of hair on top of its head. Draw pupils in its eyes.

3. Attach two back legs.

4. Erase the unneeded lines. Shade the Barimite, including its underbelly, hair, and pupils.

Qishiant

THE QISHIANT (PRONOUNCED KISH-EE-UNT) NOT ONLY USES
ITS LONG LIMBS TO MOVE AROUND ITS ROCKY PLANET,
BUT IT GRABS HOLD OF ITS ENEMIES WITH THEM.

1. Begin by drawing this alien's jelly-bean shaped head. Add its eyes and mouth.

2. Next, sketch the two sections of its body. Add its large pupils and the wrinkles above its eyes.

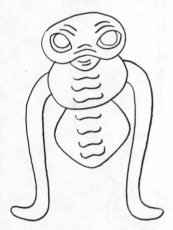

3. Sketch wrinkly lines on its two body sections. Add wrinkles to its face and mouth. Then draw the Qishiant's long limbs.

4. Further detail its eyes, and add segment lines to the limbs.

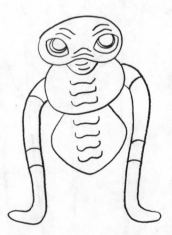

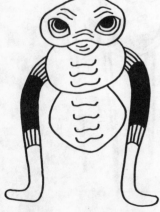

5. Complete your Qishiant by detailing and shading as shown.

Mantilid

WITH SIMPLE GEOMETRIC SHAPES, YOU CAN CREATE THIS SMALL BUT SLIMY MANTILID ALIEN!

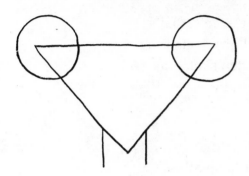

1. Draw a triangle with three equal sides for the Mantilid's head. Add two lines for its neck and large circles for its eyes.

2. Sketch a horizontal line through each eye. These are its eyelids. Next, begin to create the slime dripping down its neck.

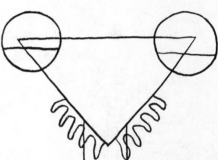

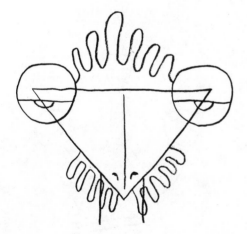

3. Draw a vertical line down the center of the Mantilid's head, and then sketch two small nostrils on either side. Insert the pupils in its eyes. Add slime spurting out of the top of the Mantilid's head.

4. Erase the unneeded lines. To complete your alien, add slime splotches on its face, and shade as shown.

7

Yetterbai

THIS HAPPY-GO-LUCKY ALIEN IS WELCOME ON ANY PLANET.

1. Begin by drawing the Yetterbai's small circular head. Insert its large open mouth, and then sketch its long, thin neck.

2. Add a mouthful of teeth, as well as a small rounded collar at the base of the neck.

3. Draw its large teardrop-shaped body, and then attach arms and legs.

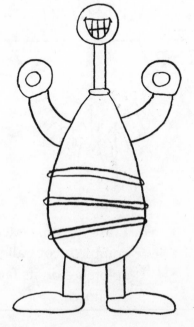

4. Sketch hands and feet, and add the bands around the Yetterbai's body. Insert the circles on the palms of its hands. These are the alien's eyes!

8

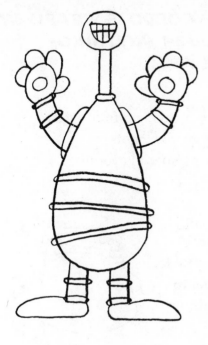

5. Continue to add detail, inserting bands on its arms, shoulders, and legs. Add four chubby fingers to each hand.

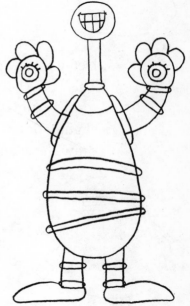

6. Draw pupils inside its eyeballs, and then accent with eyelashes. Sketch the small curved line across the chest.

7. Erase the unneeded lines, and then color and detail as shown.

Gordo

SEE THAT COOL-LOOKING EYEPIECE THE GORDO IS WEARING? WITH IT, THIS ALIEN CAN SEE THROUGH ANYTHING— WATER, WALLS . . . EVEN YOU!

I. Create the Gordo's body by drawing a four-sided shape with a rounded bottom. Sketch its two small arms, and then draw its special eyepiece.

2. Detail the eyepiece by adding a thin rectangle. This is the lens. Now draw two small circles for the palms of the Gordo's hands and a wide, slightly down-turned mouth. Don't forget to draw the small dimple beneath the mouth.

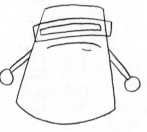

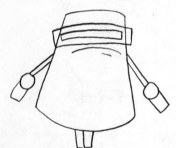

3. Complete the outline of its hands with rectangular shapes on the ends of the circles. Add two short legs.

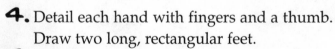

4. Detail each hand with fingers and a thumb. Draw two long, rectangular feet.

5. To finish, add antennae on top of the Gordo's head, spots on its body, and toe lines on its feet. Shade the eyepiece, and erase the unneeded lines.

Igneoid

THE IGNEOID SPENDS ITS DAYS UNDERGROUND ON THE VERY DISTANT PLANET OF IGNEOIA.

1. Draw a rounded shape for the alien's body, and insert its two circular eyes. Then draw another circular ring around each eye.

2. Attach thick arms and stubby legs. Connect its eyes with three small lines.

3. Add the Igneoid's large toes and fingers.

4. Draw some scales on the alien's head and body.

5. Continue to add more scales around the Igneoid's head. Erase the unneeded lines.

Aurigaen

THE AURIGAEN COMES FROM A PLANET INHABITED ALMOST ENTIRELY BY FEMALES.

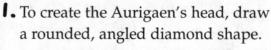

1. To create the Aurigaen's head, draw a rounded, angled diamond shape.

2. Add a thin eye and mouth. Sketch the alien's neck.

3. Draw wrinkles around its eye, and add a slit for its ear.

4. Sketch a couple of wrinkles around the ear. Then draw one of the Aurigaen's three horns.

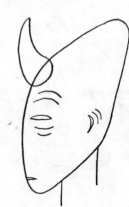

5. Add the other two horns.

6. Erase the unneeded lines in the horns and neck. To complete your Aurigaen, shade as shown. Be sure to add the lines on the horns and the spots on top of this space creature's head.

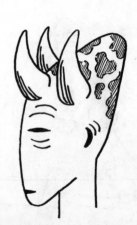

Retinoid

EVEN WITH ITS LARGE EYE, THE RETINOID CANNOT SEE FARTHER THAN 10 FEET IN FRONT OF IT!

1. Begin by drawing a circle. Inside the circle, draw the Retinoid's large eye. Add its iris and the expression lines above and below the eye.

2. Insert its pupil, and draw its long rounded body. Give the Retinoid long feet and arms.

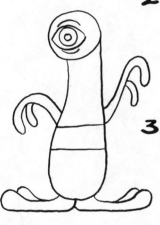

3. Add a second set of arms and feet. Draw the belt on the Retinoid's uniform.

4. Sketch the alien's open-mouthed grin, and insert the small dimple under its mouth. Detail its belt.

5. Erase the unneeded lines, and shade the Retinoid.

Zygion

ZYGIONS CAN RULE ANY PLANET THEY WANT! FORTUNATELY, THEY HAVE NO INTEREST IN EARTH.

1. To begin, draw a tilted oval for the alien's head. Add a slanted line down the center, and draw a curved *V* shape for the top of its eyes.

2. Insert its sinister-looking eyes and the top half of its body.

3. Create a rectangle for the lower half of its body.

4. Outline the alien's arms with a thin *T* shape. Then sketch a puddle of goo underneath it.

5. Define the alien's robe with thin vertical lines.

6. Finally, add decorative details to the robe. Shade the Zygion's eyes and the puddle as illustrated.

Lorta

THE LORTA FLOATS FROM STAR TO STAR, USING ITS SHARP SPIKES TO PROTECT ITSELF FROM OUTER SPACE DEBRIS.

1. Begin by drawing a circle. Then add the Lorta's eyes and two of its spikes.

2. Draw two more spikes on either side of its head, and then insert its nose.

3. Add its straight mouth and two of the smaller spikes.

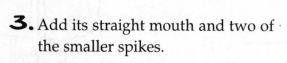

4. Sketch two more small spikes, and add four larger spikes around the edge of its head. Begin to detail its face with a chin line, eyebrows, and pupils in the eyes.

5. Finally, draw the rest of the spikes. Erase the unneeded lines, and then detail the spikes as shown. Don't forget to fill in the pupils.

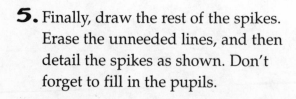

Plutonig

THIS THREE-HEADED ALIEN DOG IS A FAVORITE PET AMONG ALL PLUTONIANS.

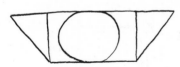

I. Begin creating your Plutonig by drawing a horizontal rectangle. Add a circle inside the rectangle for one head, and triangles on either end for its other two heads.

2. Now insert four circles for the alien dog's visible eyes. Draw a smaller rectangle underneath the first rectangle for the outline of its legs.

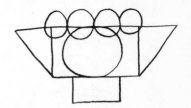

3. Begin to detail the legs by drawing lines in the smaller rectangle. Add a tiny pupil inside each eye, and then sketch a circle for each of the dog's noses. Also, insert the small circles for the dog's mouths.

4. Insert a semi-circle over the leg lines for the Plutonig's middle paw. Then draw the stem for each antenna on the top of each head.

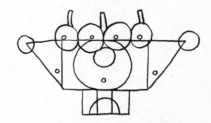

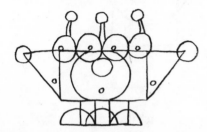

5. Add a small bulb on top of each antenna stem. Sketch its two remaining paws.

6. Erase the unneeded lines. Fill in its pupils, mouths, and noses, and then add tiny claws. Put wavy electricity lines above the antennae.

Zenlon

ALL EIGHT OF THE ZENLON'S EYES CAN LOOK IN DIFFERENT DIRECTIONS AT THE SAME TIME. THREE OF THEM CAN EVEN FLOAT SEVERAL FEET AWAY FROM THIS ALL-SEEING ALIEN.

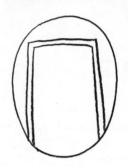

1. Begin your Zenlon by sketching its oval head. Then add two thin rules along the sides and top of the head.

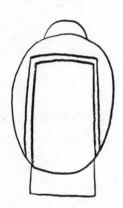

2. Draw its short neck and a small half-circle on the top of its head. This is one of the Zenlon's eyes.

3. Sketch four more half-circle eyes. Suggest shoulders.

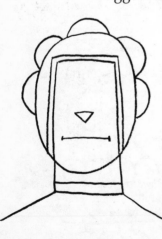

4. Insert its small triangular nose and its straight mouth. Add the thin collar between the neck and shoulders.

5. Draw a short antenna stemming from each of the five eyes.

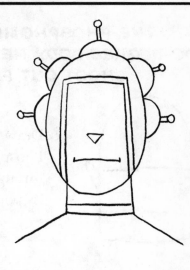

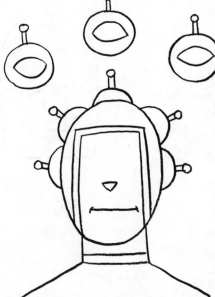

6. Next, add the Zenlon's three floating eyes. Draw three circles above its head, and then insert eyes and antennae as shown.

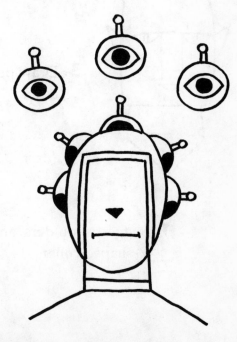

7. Add pupils, and color as shown.

Phospholing

THE PHOSPHOLING MAINTAINS ITS SCORCHING 200-DEGREE BODY HEAT WITH FLAMES THAT CONTINUALLY SHOOT OUT FROM THE TOP OF ITS HEAD.

1. Draw a rounded bullet shape for the Phospholing's head. Add a horizontal line through the center of the head, and draw its pointed ears and straight mouth.

2. Insert its rectangular nose and the small triangle under the mouth. Sketch two half-circles for its eyes.

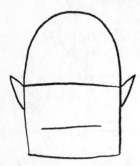

3. Draw pupils in its eyes, and add a *V*-shaped neck.

4. Suggest shoulders, and insert a *V*-shaped collar.

5. Next, add one of the flames coming from this alien's head.

6. Insert more flames on either side of its head.

7. Erase the unneeded lines inside the flames, and then darken the pupils, nose, chin, and collar. Add a few small flames shooting out from the main flames.

Syzygene

THIS GOOFY-LOOKING ALIEN IS ENDANGERED ON ITS SMALL QUAINT PLANET. IT CAN ONLY BE FOUND IN SOME OF THE PLANET'S LARGER ZOOS.

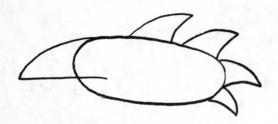

1. Draw a flattened oval for the Syzygene's head. Then sketch its long beak and four small fins.

2. Add its two bulging eyes connected to its head with thin tubes. Insert pupils, and draw small *V*-shaped fins on the side of its head.

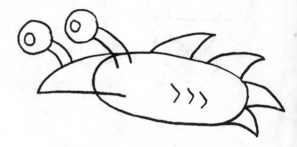

3. Sketch the Syzygene's short, round body and skinny neck. Then draw four of its long toes.

4. Lastly, draw two more toes, and fill in the pupils. Erase any unneeded lines.

Dylon-Cir

THIS ALIEN MAY LOOK VERY MUCH LIKE EARTH'S RAM,
BUT THE DYLON-CIR IS TRULY AN ALIEN CREATURE: INSTEAD OF
WALKING FROM PLACE TO PLACE, IT FLIES—TAIL FIRST!

1. Draw a slightly tilted circle for the Dylon-Cir's head. Add its one large eye and rectangular beard.

2. Sketch the eye's iris and pupil, and insert two small nostrils and a little smile. Then draw a smaller oval for the body.

3. Insert its neck, and add two large curved horns.

4. Now draw the Dylon-Cir's three near feet and its tail.

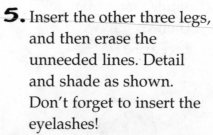

5. Insert the other three legs, and then erase the unneeded lines. Detail and shade as shown. Don't forget to insert the eyelashes!

 # Phocodon

THE IMMORTAL PHOCODON HAS RULED ITS PLANET, PHOCOS, SINCE ITS CREATION MILLIONS OF YEARS AGO.

1. Begin drawing your Phocodon by creating a finger shape for its head and neck. Then add one thin ring and one wide ring for the outline of its collar.

2. Draw its winged headpiece, and insert a band just below it. Sketch a thin line for its mouth just above the collar.

3. Insert two large rounded eyes, and begin to create the Phocodon's long robe.

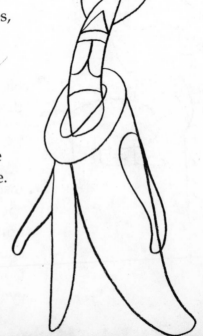

4. Detail the headpiece with a small triangle. Then sketch two long arms.

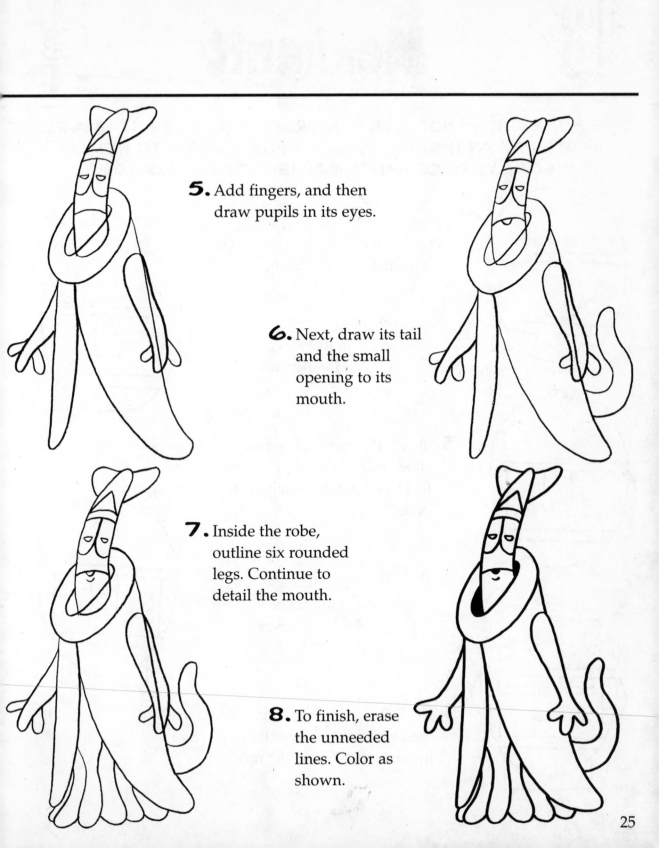

5. Add fingers, and then draw pupils in its eyes.

6. Next, draw its tail and the small opening to its mouth.

7. Inside the robe, outline six rounded legs. Continue to detail the mouth.

8. To finish, erase the unneeded lines. Color as shown.

25

Mekkanit

THE MEKKANIT IS NOT A LIVING, BREATHING ALIEN. IT IS A ROBOT CREATED BY AN INGENIOUS ALIEN POPULATION TO HELP SOLVE SOME VERY COMPLEX MATHEMATICAL PROBLEMS.

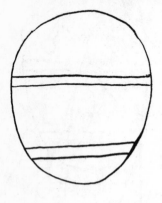

1. Begin your Mekkanit robot by drawing a circle. Then insert four horizontal lines as shown.

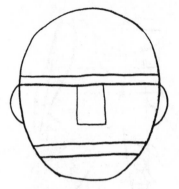

2. Add its two ears and rectangular nose.

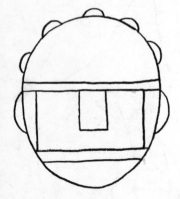

3. Sketch the vertical lines on either side of its face, and draw five small bumps along the top of its head.

4. Insert rectangles for the outlines of the Mekkanit's eyes. Draw its neck.

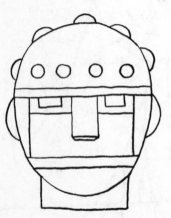

5. Next, sketch the metal circles across its forehead. Add rectangular pupils and the small line below the nose.

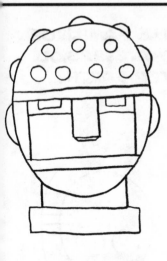

6. Add more circles on its forehead, and draw the base of the robot's neck.

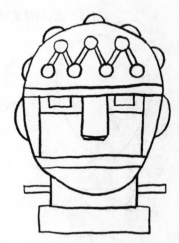

7. Connect the circles on its forehead with metal bands. Add the thin bolts sticking out from its neck.

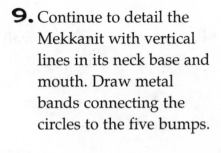

8. Sketch the antennae stemming from the bolts, and insert more metal bands on the forehead.

9. Continue to detail the Mekkanit with vertical lines in its neck base and mouth. Draw metal bands connecting the circles to the five bumps.

10. Shade the alien as shown.

27

Roswellian

DOES THIS LARGE-HEADED ALIEN LOOK A LITTLE FAMILIAR?
THE ROSWELLIAN CREATURES ARE AVID TRAVELERS,
AND MANY BELIEVE THEY HAVE EVEN VISITED EARTH.

1. First, draw an upside-down egg for the alien's head. Then sketch its small round body, complete with a waistline. Insert two large eyes.

2. Add stubby legs and arms, and then attach feet and hands.

3. Sketch a small smile and the pupils in its eyes. Also, add thumbs and another waistline. This will create a belt.

4. Give this Roswellian small eyebrows, and begin to detail its space suit as shown. Be sure to add cuff lines at the wrists and ankles.

5. Finally, add lines on each of the cuffs, and erase the lines in the thumbs. Then color as shown. If you want, you could even create a funky spaceship that this alien can use for its travels.

Flittling

THIS ALIEN LOVES TO FLIT ABOUT ITS PLANET, FLOTT, PLAYING HIDE-AND-SEEK WITH OTHER FLITTLINGS.

1. Draw a bean-shaped head, which will include the Flittling's beak. Add a tiny nostril and its large visible eye.

2. Sketch four rectangular feathers on its head, and insert a pupil and eyelid.

3. Draw the Flittling's long neck and pear-shaped body. Then complete its mouth by drawing a lower jaw.

4. Sketch the four feathers on its lower back and its two arms with paws.

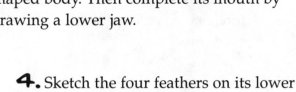

5. Next, attach the Flittling's legs and feet.

6. To finish, erase the unneeded lines. Also, color in the pupil, and insert claw lines in the hands and feet.

Sauroid

JUST LIKE A FISH SWIMS GRACEFULLY THROUGH WATER, THE SAUROID GLIDES IN THE GREEN, GOOEY LIQUID THAT COVERS ITS PLANET.

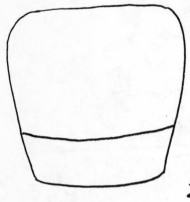

I. To begin, draw its squarish body shape, and then insert a horizontal line for its waist.

2. Add a half-circle on top of the body for its forehead. Sketch its small nose.

3. Draw large eyebrows coming out from either side of the Sauroid's nose. Then sketch its thick upper lip.

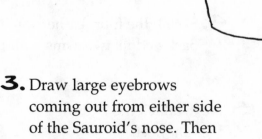

4. Complete the mouth with a fat lower lip. Add eyes beneath its eyebrows and definition lines on its torso.

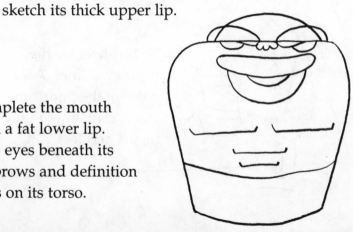

5. Attach arms and legs.

6. Next, create the Sauroid's strong fins. Also, add its thumbs and feet.

7. Erase the unneeded lines. Add finishing details, and then color the pupils and mouth.

Venusian

THE VENUSIAN'S THREE SUCTIONED FEET HELP IT MANEUVER AROUND ITS PLANET, VENUS.

1. To begin, draw a half-circle for the top of its head. Add two rounded horns. Then insert its eyes and big open mouth.

2. Add three more horns of varying sizes. Then sketch eyebrows.

3. Draw the Venusian's three legs with suctioned feet.

4. Erase the unneeded lines, add finishing details, and color.

CORNEOIDS MAY NOT BE ABLE TO TALK—THEY HAVE NO MOUTHS— BUT THEY SURE HAVE NO PROBLEM SEEING!

1. Begin by drawing a bunch of overlapping circles to create the Corneoid's eyes. When you are done, your drawing should look like a cluster of grapes.

2. Start to add pupils in the eyes.

3. Add the rest of the pupils, and then sketch the Corneoid's two short antennae.

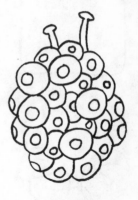

4. Draw the legs and feet.

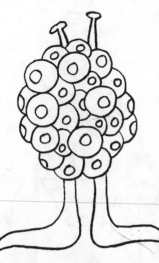

5. To finish, add two more feet, and color in each pupil.

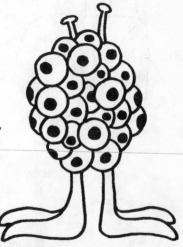

Biagene

EVERY MEMBER OF THE BIAGENE SPECIES IS BORN WITH AT LEAST TWO HEADS. AS THEY GET OLDER, THEY MAY GROW MORE HEADS. THEY COULD EVEN END UP WITH AS MANY AS FIFTEEN HEADS!

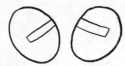

1. Begin by drawing the two oval heads. Insert the Biagene's two rectangular eye shields, and sketch its squarish torso.

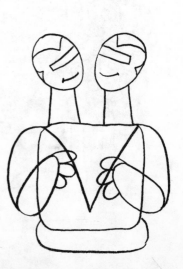

2. Draw its necks and two arms.

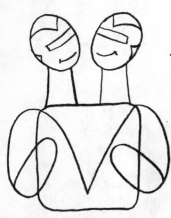

3. Complete the arms, and begin to add details. Draw the large *V* on its torso, and insert angular hairlines on its heads. Don't forget the two mouths.

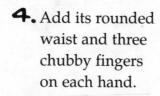

4. Add its rounded waist and three chubby fingers on each hand.

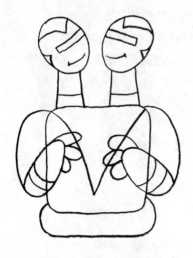

5. Sketch its neck- and wristbands.

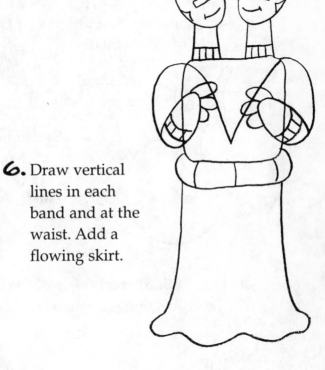

6. Draw vertical lines in each band and at the waist. Add a flowing skirt.

7. Erase the unneeded lines, and then add finishing details as shown.

Xiphion

**WITH THE HELP OF ITS ROBOTIC TORSO,
THE DEADLY XIPHION FLIES AROUND ITS PLANET
SHOOTING DEADLY RAYS AT ITS ENEMIES.**

1. Draw an upside-down teardrop for the Xiphion's head. Add its two large eyes, one only partially showing.

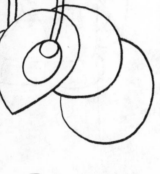

2. Sketch the pupil inside its front eye, and then attach antennae to both eyes. Add two rounded body parts.

3. Draw a third body segment as well as the visible segments of its arms.

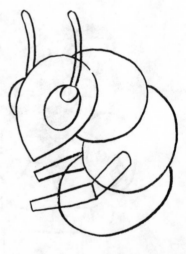

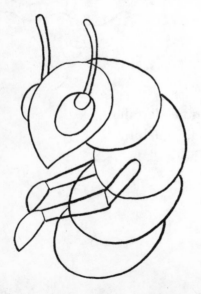

4. Outline its hand pincers, and draw one more body segment.

5. Attach a rounded base to the last body segment. Then add small lines inside its hands to define the pincers. Add a joint piece at the top of the near arm.

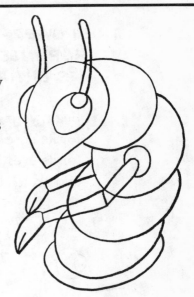

6. Outline the Xiphion's robotic base. Add joint pieces at its elbow and wrists.

7. Sketch the mechanical details of the alien's robotic base.

8. Erase the unneeded lines. Last, detail and color as shown.

Taraxacum

THE POWERFUL FEET OF THE TARAXACUM HELP IT TO HOP MILES AT A TIME. IT CAN TRAVEL AROUND ITS ENTIRE PLANET IN JUST A FEW HOURS.

1. Begin your Taraxacum by drawing an oval for its nose and mouth area and a small circle for its eye. Attach a crescent moon to the eye, and sketch three tiny gills.

2. Sketch a large bulging pupil inside the eye, and add its nostril and smiling mouth. Then connect the eye to the mouth area with a long, curved stem.

3. Add a curved chin under its mouth, and draw a circle for its body.

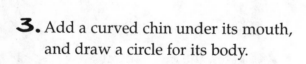

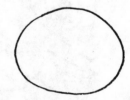

4. Insert a long, thin neck, and draw its visible upper thigh. Add eyelashes to the eye.

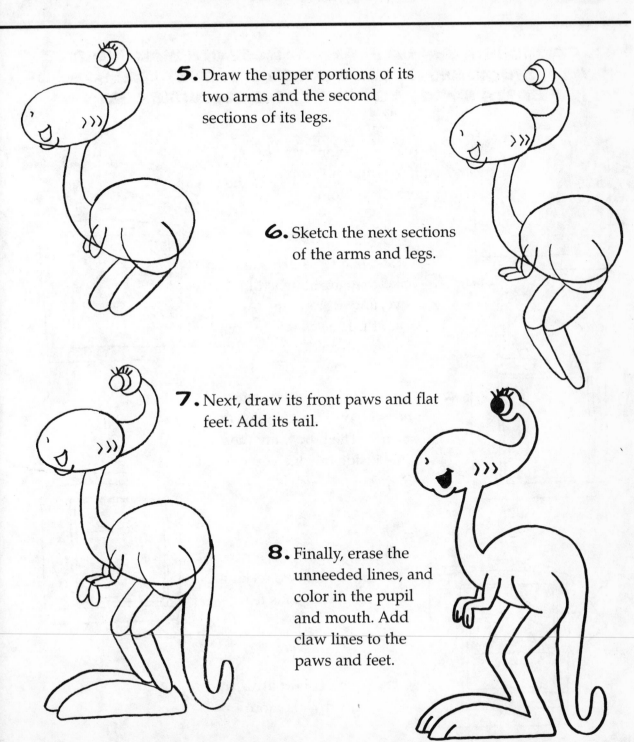

5. Draw the upper portions of its two arms and the second sections of its legs.

6. Sketch the next sections of the arms and legs.

7. Next, draw its front paws and flat feet. Add its tail.

8. Finally, erase the unneeded lines, and color in the pupil and mouth. Add claw lines to the paws and feet.

Zolon

CAN YOU IMAGINE A PLANET FILLED WITH WALKING TVS? WELL, THE ALIENS ON ZOLONIOUS LOOK JUST LIKE SOME OF EARTH'S MOST SOPHISTICATED TELEVISION SETS.

1. Begin your Zolon by drawing a square with a horizontal line across the bottom.

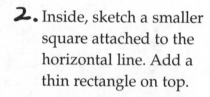

2. Inside, sketch a smaller square attached to the horizontal line. Add a thin rectangle on top.

3. Attach two smaller rectangles on either side of the rectangle you just drew. Then draw another square inside the one you created in Step 2.

4. Add squinty eyes, a nose, and two rectangles for the Zylon's legs.

5. Suggest short arms, and draw a wide mouth.

6. Add cuffs to the arms and the circular antennae to the top of the Zolon. Complete the nose, and add a chin.

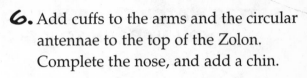

7. Attach the long, straight antenna to the top. Then sketch the rounded hands and feet.

8. Detail the antennae. Add fingers to the hands, and outline the soles of the Zolon's shoes.

9. Finally, erase the unneeded lines in the hands and the middle antenna. Add finishing details, and shade as shown.

Lucanite

YOU BETTER WATCH OUT FOR THIS DANGEROUS WARRIOR ALIEN IF YOU HAPPEN TO VISIT THE PLANET LUCAN.

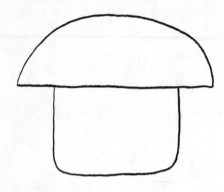

1. First, draw a half-circle for the Lucanite's helmet. Attach a rounded square.

2. Add two circles to the square, and draw a curved horn inside each one.

3. Under the helmet, create three small half-circles for its eyes. Then draw two more partial circles attached to the original ones.

4. Add a wavy line between the Lucanite's eyes and horns. Suggest a short neck.

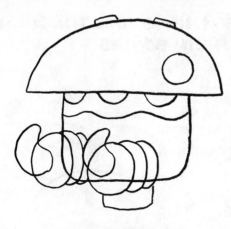

5. Draw rectangular bases for the Lucanite's lightning-shaped antennae. Add a circle on its helmet.

6. Draw the antennae, and add its collar at the base of its neck.

7. Further detail the helmet. Add pupils in its eyes, and suggest shoulders.

8. Finish detailing the helmet, erase the unneeded lines, and color as shown.

Xenobyte

XENOBYTES DO NOT HAVE NOSES. THEY SMELL THROUGH THE SPOTS ALL OVER THEIR BODIES.

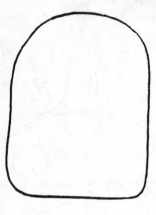

1. Draw a rounded rectangle for the Xenobyte's head.

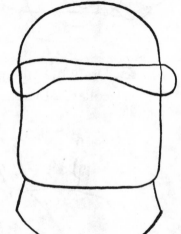

2. Sketch a curved band for its single eyebrow, and then add its thick neck.

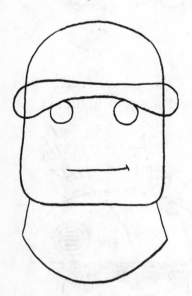

3. Draw two circular eyes, and add a straight mouth.

4. Insert a few wrinkle lines above its eyebrow. Draw two circles for the buttons on its clothing.

5. Begin to add the spots on its head and neck. Further render the buttons on its clothing.

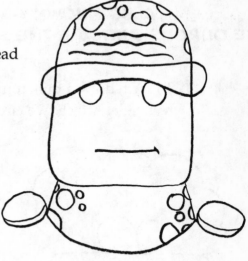

6. Create the top of the Xenobyte's robe, attached to the two buttons.

7. Finish your alien by coloring in the spots and eyes, and detailing the buttons.

Ourousian

**ALSO KNOWN AS THE "LIVING BRAINS,"
THE OUROUSIANS ARE THE SMARTEST BEINGS IN THE GALAXY.**

I. To start, draw a thin, rounded rectangle. Attach two circles for eyes.

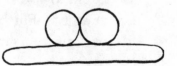

2. Then begin to outline the brain, drawing puffy shapes as shown.

3. Add the detail lines within the brain. For the Ourousian's thin body, create a puffy shape that extends down from the head. Draw three thin, flowing tails. Add pupils to the eyes.

4. Detail the Ourousian as shown, and fill in the pupils.

Pleuronectoid

A POPULAR PET AMONG MANY DIFFERENT ALIEN SPECIES, THIS GENTLE ALIEN FEEDS ON SUNLIGHT.

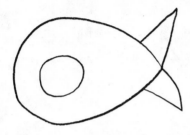

1. Begin by drawing the fishlike outline of the Pleuronectoid's body. Then insert one of its large eyes.

2. Draw three more eyes floating above its body.

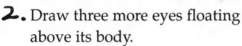
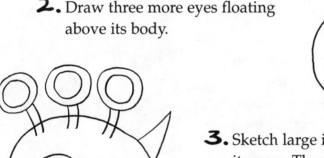

3. Sketch large irises inside all of its eyes. Then attach the three floating eyes to its body.

4. Draw small pupils inside the irises, and add its small fin.

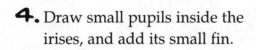

5. Erase the unneeded lines. Then add finishing details, including eyelashes. Partially color in the pupils.

Zwydactoid

EVEN THOUGH THEY HAVE LARGE MOUTHS, THE ZWYDACTOIDS COMMUNICATE THROUGH THEIR ANTENNAE, NOT BY TALKING.

1. Begin by drawing the rounded outlines of the Zwydactoid's head and body.

2. Add the lower portion of its mouth, including the outline of its tongue. Insert the circular antenna base on the top of its head, and outline its belly.

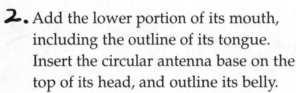

3. Draw the thin antenna and the line extending from it to the top of the Zwydactoid's mouth. Sketch the first segments of its arms.

4. Create its triangular eyebrows and the second segments of its arms.

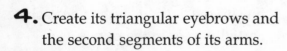

5. Below the eyebrows, draw its triangular eyes. Attach the first of the three sets of claws below its belly.

6. Complete its eyes. Then add its hands and the other two sets of claws.

7. Next, add the feathers on the Zwydactoid's back and elbows. Draw the lines on its belly.

8. Erase the unneeded lines, and color as shown.

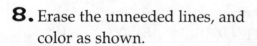

Ix

ALIENS FROM THE DARK NEBULA, THE IX
CANNOT SURVIVE IN TOO MUCH SUNLIGHT.

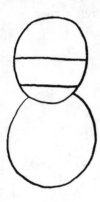

1. Draw the circular outlines of the Ix's head and body. Then create the wide band across its head.

2. Insert its eyes and mouth.

3. Sketch pupils in its eyes and a feather coming out from its headband.

4. Add two more feathers, and sketch its uneven eyebrows. Also draw the X on its body. This will be the outline for the Ix's clothing.

5. Continue to add feathers, and draw arms and legs.

6. Draw the remaining feathers on the Ix's head. Attach the second segments of its arms. Then add feet and a tail.

7. Sketch its hands and the feathers on the end of its tail.

8. To finish your drawing, erase the unneeded lines. Then add details, such as the wrist- and anklebands, and the lines in the feathers. Also, color as shown.

Hephaestoid

THIS METHANE-EATER NEVER NEEDS TO USE A FLASHLIGHT. INSTEAD, IT LIGHTS ITS WAY WITH ITS BLAZING SCALP.

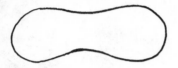

1. Begin by drawing this alien's eye shield.

2. Then attach the bottom part of its head. Insert its nose and the circle in the middle of its eye shield.

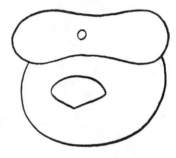

3. Insert the scales above its nose, and draw its down-turned mouth.

4. Add the pointed scales on either side of the nose and the triangular chin.

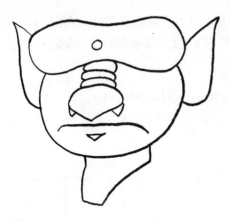

5. Draw pointy ears and a neck.

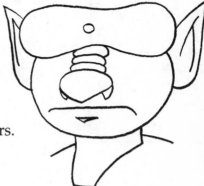

6. Detail the ears, and suggest shoulders.

7. Next, add some of the flames shooting out from the top of this fiery alien's head.

8. Create the rest of the flames. Shade as shown, but don't forget to add the shadow beneath the Hephaestoid's eye shield.

Muoning

ONLY THREE INCHES TALL, THE MUONINGS TRAVEL IN ROBOTIC BODY ARMOR THAT IS SIX FEET TALL.

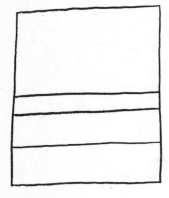

1. Draw the square outline of the Muoning's armor. Insert three horizontal lines as shown.

2. Divide two of the horizontal lines drawn in Step 1 with a vertical line. Draw a small square at the top of the armor to outline the chest.

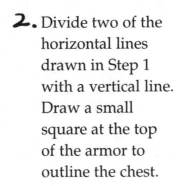

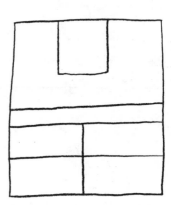

3. Add four thin rectangles as shown. These are the control panels on the Muoning's robotic armor.

4. Attach a half-circle for its headpiece and two narrow rectangles for the base of the armor's arms.

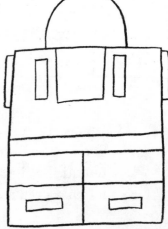

5. Draw a thin band across the headpiece, and insert a smaller square inside the chest outline. Next, add the eyes and mouth, as well as the circular knobs inside the control panels.

6. Further detail the face with three vertical lines to create metal plates. Sketch the arms.

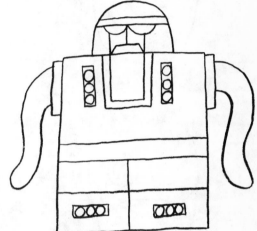

7. Continue to insert metal plate lines as shown.

8. Finally, complete your Muoning by coloring as shown.

Beastion

 1

THIS ALIEN MAY LOOK LIKE EARTH'S LION, BUT UNLIKE A LION, IT DOES NOT HAVE A BODY!

1. Draw the head outline, and insert eyes.

2. Then begin to shape the head by drawing the curved lines inside the outline. Add a big nose.

3. Draw eyebrows and its crescent-shaped pupils.

4. Sketch the furry mane around its head.

5. To finish your Beastion, detail the fur, and color as shown.

Raioid

THE RAIOID CAN TRAVEL THROUGH BOTH SPACE AND TIME!

1. Draw the oval outline of the Raioid's head. Insert its circular eyes.

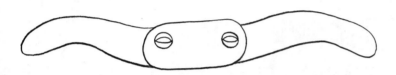

2. Attach the first set of long arms, and outline its pupils.

3. Create the outline of its mouth, and draw the next set of arms.

4. Draw the hump suggesting the Raioid's back. Also, attach the last set of arms.

5. To finish, insert scale lines on each of the arms, color in the pupils, and add eyebrows.

Ailuron

THIS FELINE-TYPE ALIEN FROM THE PLANET SEERON IS ONE OF THE MOST INTELLIGENT BEINGS IN THE UNIVERSE.

1. Draw the Ailuron's circular head. Attach ears, and insert the outline of its one large eye.

2. Create the outlines of its cheeks extending from either side of its eye. Then insert its jaw between the cheeks. Add antennae.

3. Draw a mouth in the jaw, and begin to detail its eye.

4. Further detail its eye, and draw whiskers coming out from its cheeks. Add a neck.

5. Draw the outline of its body, and begin to create its legs.

6. Add the second section of one of its front legs.

7. Draw the second section of the other front leg, and add its tail.

8. Next, create the two pairs of back legs.

9. Erase the unneeded lines, and then add fur lines on the ends of the legs and tail. Don't forget to color in the tongue.

Sarosite

THE SAROSITES USE ROCKETS TO MOVE AROUND BECAUSE THERE IS VERY LITTLE GRAVITY ON THE PLANET SAROS.

1. Begin by drawing the rounded square for the Sarosite's body.

2. Add its eye shield and mouth.

3. Draw its chin and the curved shape around the eye shield.

4. Outline its eyebrows, and draw the first section of its rocket.

5. Add the second part of the rocket. Then draw the eye shield bands on either side of the shield. Begin to create the antenna with a thin triangle.

6. Further detail the antenna, and add three small rectangles at the bottom of the base.

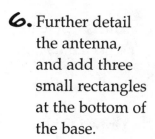

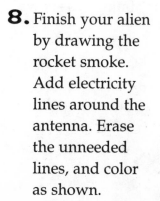

7. Attach ears, and draw the lines in the Sarosite's base and eyebands.

8. Finish your alien by drawing the rocket smoke. Add electricity lines around the antenna. Erase the unneeded lines, and color as shown.

Xeeexxx

THE XEEEXXX COMMUNICATES ITS MOOD BY CHANGING THE COLOR OF ITS STRIPE.

I. Draw the egg-shaped outline of the Xeeexxx's body. Then insert eyes, complete with pupils. Attach ears.

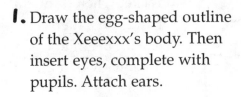

2. Add the lines inside its ears, and sketch its nose.

3. Draw its mouth and nostrils. Then attach two legs.

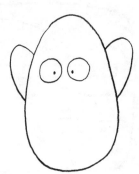

4. Add three more legs, and draw the stripe down the center of this alien's body. Also, add the warty bumps as shown.

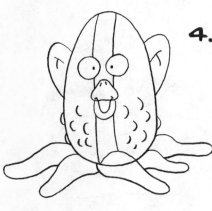

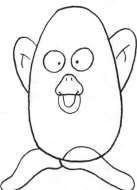

5. Erase the unneeded lines. Detail and color your Xeeexxx as illustrated.

Cannamite

THIS ALIEN DRINKS WITH ITS RIGHT MOUTH AND EATS WITH ITS LEFT ONE!

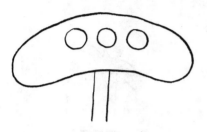

1. Draw a pickle shape for the Cannamite's head. Insert three circular eyes and its long, thin neck.

2. At the base of its neck, draw its circular body. Also, draw its two noses.

3. Add curved lines for the mouths, and attach two legs with feet to the body. Add pupils.

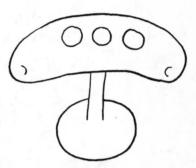

4. Draw two more sets of legs and feet.

5. Erase the unneeded lines. Add a tail, and also a tuft of hair on the top of the Cannamite's head. Fill in the hair and pupils.

Asparagand

THE SUPER-SOPHISTICATED ASPARAGANDS ARE THE UNIVERSE'S ONLY INTELLIGENT PLANT LIFE.

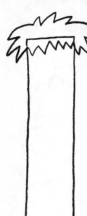

1. Draw a long vertical rectangle for the Asparagand's body. Then add hair.

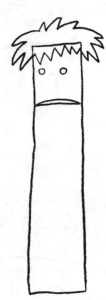

2. Insert its eyes and mouth.

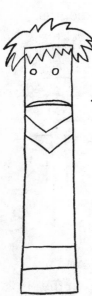

3. Next, add its *V*-shaped chest and the band at the bottom of its body.

4. Attach arms, and draw the lines beneath its eyes.

5. Sketch its four
eyebrows and
three feet.

6. Add the vertical lines
on its chin, and draw
its fingers.

7. To complete your
Asparagand,
erase unneeded
lines. Detail and
color as shown.

Egghead

EGGHEADS CAN FLY FASTER THAN THE SPEED OF LIGHT.

1. Draw a stubby egg shape for the Egghead's body. Add one triangular antenna and two eyes.

2. Add two more antennae, as well as its eyebrows, nose, and mouth.

3. Attach balls to the tops of the antennae. Then outline its face, and sketch pupils in its eyes.

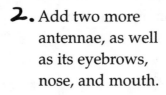

4. Further detail its antennae. Draw the circle beneath its face. This is a bright light that helps the Egghead see as it flies through the galaxy.

5. Complete detailing
its antennae, and
add another outline
around its face
and light source.

6. Draw lines above its nose,
and suggest the chin.
Sketch the rectangular
shapes on either side of
its light.

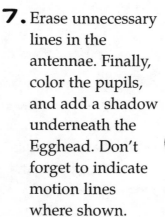

7. Erase unnecessary
lines in the
antennae. Finally,
color the pupils,
and add a shadow
underneath the
Egghead. Don't
forget to indicate
motion lines
where shown.

Phloxoid

THIS SEVEN-FOOT-TALL INSECTOID LIVES AMONG THE ASTEROID BELTS OF SPACE.

1. Begin by drawing the round head and three eyes of the Phloxoid.

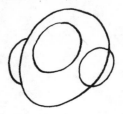

2. Add its long snout, slightly curved at the end. Also, begin to detail its eyes with curved lines.

3. Sketch the three long ears extending from the top of its head. Add the opening at the end of its snout.

4. Add its neck and body.

5. Draw a collar around its neck, and attach the first two leg segments.

6. Sketch its wings and the second leg segments.

7. Next, add the clawed feet. Draw the sharp spikes shooting out from the backs of its knees.

8. Finish the Phloxoid by erasing the unneeded lines, and detailing its wings and snout.

THE KREE-LAN HAS THE AMAZING ABILITY TO HYPNOTIZE ANY LIVING CREATURE WITH ITS THIRD EYE.

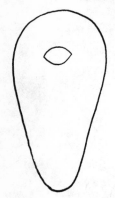

1. Create the outline of its head by drawing an elongated egg shape. Then insert what will be the large third eye, which rests on the Kree-lan's forehead.

2. Draw a thin horizontal line beneath this eye, and add a large open mouth.

3. Create the alien's other two squinting eyes by adding a sideways *V* at either side of the horizontal line. Draw three curved lines to suggest its nose.

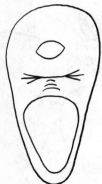

4. Further detail its face by adding a pupil to the third eye and eyebrows above all the eyes. Also, draw its sharp pointed teeth.

5. Sketch ears, and add a neck with shoulders.

6. To complete your drawing, color in each of its eyebrows and the pupil.

Belion

THIS SHY LITTLE ALIEN ORIGINALLY LIVED ON MARS BUT MIGRATED TO THE MUCH COOLER PLANET OF BELOS 650,000 YEARS AGO.

1. Begin to create your Belion by drawing two ovals: one for its head and one for its body. Connect the ovals with a neck. Then add its eyes, mouth, and leg joints.

2. Complete its mouth with a lower lip. Draw pupils in its eyes, as well as the first of the three pairs of long horns extending from its head. Add the leg segments.

3. Insert its nostrils, and sketch a pair of horns coming out of the Belion's body. Add its tail and feet.

4. Create the rest of the head and body horns. Draw toes on its feet.

5. Erase the unneeded lines, and then color and detail your drawing as shown.

Valkonin

HIGHLY POWERFUL BEINGS, VALKONINS USE THEIR IMMENSE BRAINS TO CONTROL THE WEATHER ON THEIR PLANET.

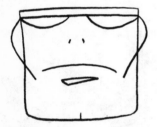

1. Draw a squarish shape for this Valkonin's head. Then insert a narrow headband at the top and a small vertical line at the bottom of its head.

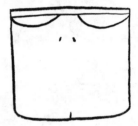

2. Add its eyes and nostrils.

3. Draw its mouth, chin cleft, and ears.

4. Create the outline of the alien's very large brain.

5. Begin to detail its brain, and add the neckline around its head.

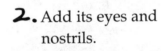

6. Further detail its brain. Also, suggest shoulders.

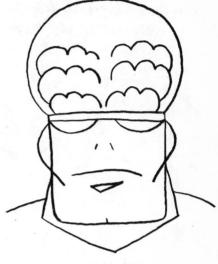

7. Finish the brain, and then add the three antennae on top of its head. Add a collar around its neck.

8. To complete your Valkonin, erase the unneeded lines. Then add the electricity shooting out of the alien's head. Shade and detail as shown.

Tantalite

EVEN WITH ITS AERODYNAMIC SHAPE, THREE LEGS, AND TWO WINGS, THE TANTALITE MOVES VERY, VERY SLOWLY.

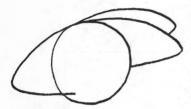

1. Outline the alien's head with a circle. On the left side, draw its snout. On the right side, draw its two ears.

2. Add the visible triangular eye and the visible nostril.

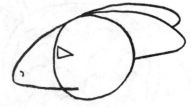

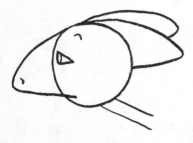

3. Further detail its eye by creating the pupil. Add its visible eyebrow and skinny neck.

4. Attach the circular body to its neck.

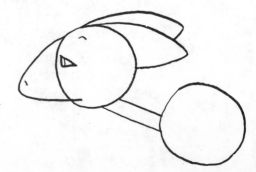

5. Add its three legs with feet.

6. Draw the outlines of its toes, and attach the wings to its body.

7. Finally, erase the unneeded lines, and add the shaded spots on the Tantalite's ears and wings. Also, color in the pupil.

Xystos

3

WITH ELECTRICITY FLOWING AROUND ITS HEAD AND THROUGH ITS VEINS, THIS ALIEN IS A REAL SHOCKER!

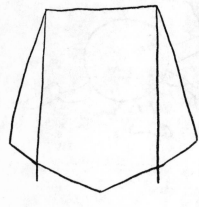

1. Begin by drawing a pentagon (five-sided shape). Then draw two vertical lines down either side of this shape.

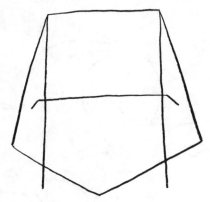

2. Sketch the Xystos's horizontal waistline as shown.

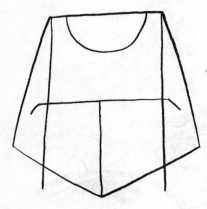

3. Add its neckline, and draw a vertical line extending from its waistline.

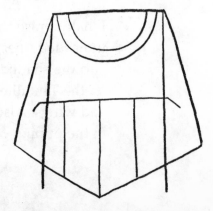

4. Create a collar around its neck, and add more lines extending from its waist.

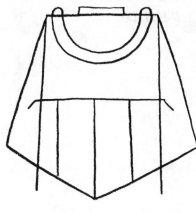

5. Attach a neck, and extend the collar above its shoulders.

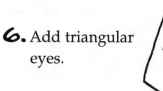

6. Add triangular eyes.

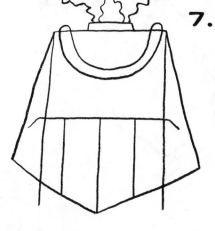

7. Draw the Xystos's head, which is made up entirely of electric bolts. Be sure to outline its mouth as well.

8. Erase the unneeded lines, and add electric wires and bolts of electricity as shown.

RHIZOMORPHS HAVE THE ABILITY TO ROCKET THEMSELVES FROM PLANET TO PLANET.

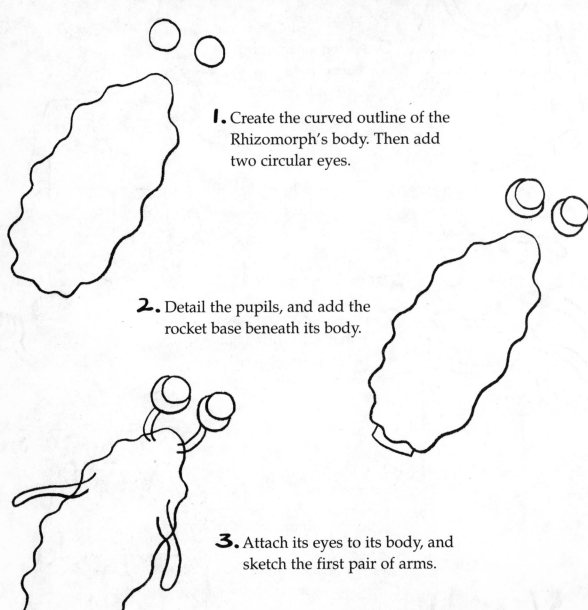

1. Create the curved outline of the Rhizomorph's body. Then add two circular eyes.

2. Detail the pupils, and add the rocket base beneath its body.

3. Attach its eyes to its body, and sketch the first pair of arms.

4. Add more arms, and further detail its eyes.

5. Next, draw the slimy goop that covers the Rhizomorph's body. Add another half-circle inside each eye.

6. To finish, erase the unneeded lines, and color in the pupils. Last, add the rocket smoke shooting out from the bottom of this unusual alien.

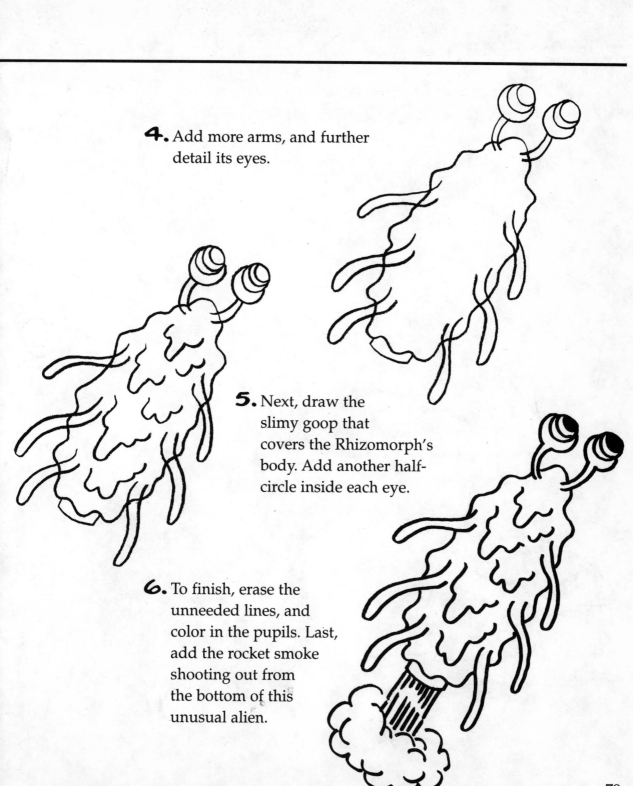